Table of Contents

So What's a Cake Pop?

Cake pops are bite-size treats made of crumbled cake mixed with frosting and covered in candy coating. They're very easy to make—especially when you use cake mixes and prepared frosting—and decorating them can be as simple or as challenging as you want. Just read through the tips below to help you get started.

Ingredients for Sweet Success

• You can use any kind of cake to make cake pops—use your favorite 13×9-inch cake recipe instead of a mix if you prefer. You may want to bake the cake a day ahead of time since it needs to be completely cool before crumbling.

• The frosting, like the cake, can be homemade or store-bought. Homemade buttercream and cream cheese frostings work well, and if you make your own frosting, you can use less sugar to balance the sweetness in the cake and the candy coating. But canned frostings (any variety except whipped) are a convenient option with many different flavors to choose from.

• Candy coating can be found in a wide variety of colors and flavors at craft and specialty stores. (You might have already seen it in its basic chocolate and vanilla or almond versions in the supermarket, where it's called bark or confectionary coating.) Candy coating should be stored in a cool, dry place at room temperature, never refrigerated or frozen.

1-2-3 Pop!

1. The first step in making cake pops is crumbling the cake. It's easy to crumble cake with your hands, but you can also use a food processor to do the job. You should end up with fine crumbs and no large cake pieces remaining.

2. Next, mix in the frosting. Again, it's easiest to do this with your hands, but a spoon or spatula works well if you don't want to get your hands messy. The mixture should be moist enough to roll into balls, but not so wet or heavy that the balls won't hold their shape.

3. Finally, roll the mixture into balls or other shapes with your hands and put them on a waxed paper-lined baking sheet. Cover and refrigerate for a few hours until they're firm.

Dipping & Decorating

• To transform a ball of cake and frosting into irresistible edible art, you need plenty of candy coating. Place the coating in a deep microwavable container (drinking glasses work well) and microwave on MEDIUM (50%) for 1 minute. Stir, then microwave for additional 30-second intervals until the coating is completely melted, stirring after each interval. Be careful not to overheat the coating. It's best to use the coating as is, especially when you're first getting started, but if you find the coating to be too thick, you can thin it slightly by adding a small amount of vegetable oil or shortening. Heating the coating longer won't make it any thinner.

• For each cake pop, dip a lollipop stick about ½ inch into the melted candy coating, then insert the stick into the cake ball (no more than halfway through). After a few minutes to set, the cake pops can be dipped.

• Before you start dipping, make sure you have your decorations and a foam block nearby. (Floral foam blocks work particularly well.) If you'll be adding decorations you want to adhere to the cake pops while the coating is wet (for example, the ears on the Funky Monkeys, page 14), you have a short window of time (about a minute) to arrange these candies on the pops before the coating sets. But if you aren't able to attach the decorations at this point, don't worry. The melted coating acts as a very strong glue, and you can simply use a toothpick to place dots of coating on the pop wherever you want to attach your candies. Hold them in place until the coating sets.

Cake Pop Pointers

• For recipes with lighter coatings, it's best to choose lighter cakes and frostings so the cake doesn't show through.

• If you put your cake pops in the freezer rather than the refrigerator to firm them up quickly, make sure they don't freeze solid (or if they do, let them warm up a little before dipping). The warm melted coating doesn't work as well on frozen surfaces.

• If you don't find the color of candy coating you want, you can combine different color coatings to create a new shade. You can also tint the coating with candy coloring, but be sure to use oil-based candy coloring and not regular food coloring.

• Arranging small sprinkles and decors on a little cake pop can be frustrating. Try using tweezers to place the decorations exactly where you want them—you can find inexpensive tweezers at craft stores.

Critter Pops

Fun Frogs
Makes about 24 pops

½ baked and cooled 13×9-inch cake*
½ cup plus 2 tablespoons frosting
1 package (14 to 16 ounces) green candy coating
24 lollipop sticks
　Foam block
　White fruit-flavored pastel candy wafers
　Chocolate sprinkles
　Black string licorice, cut into 1¼-inch lengths
　Black decorator frosting

Prepare a cake from a mix according to package directions or use your favorite recipe. Cake must be cooled completely.

1. Line large baking sheet with waxed paper. Use hands to crumble cake into large bowl. (You should end up with fine crumbs.)

2. Add frosting to cake crumbs; mix with hands until well blended. Shape mixture into 1½-inch balls (about 2 tablespoons cake mixture per ball); place on prepared baking sheet. Cover with plastic wrap; refrigerate at least 1 hour or freeze 10 minutes to firm.

3. When cake balls are firm, place candy coating in deep microwavable bowl. Melt according to package directions. Dip one lollipop stick about ½ inch into melted coating; insert stick into cake ball (no more than halfway through). Return cake pop to baking sheet in refrigerator to set. Repeat with remaining cake balls and sticks.

4. Working with one cake pop at a time, hold stick and dip cake ball into melted coating to cover completely, letting excess coating drip off. Rotate stick gently and/or tap stick on edge of bowl, if necessary, to remove excess coating. Place cake pop in foam block. Immediately attach two candy wafers to top of pop for eyes while coating is still wet; hold in place until coating is set.

5. Dip toothpick in candy coating; place two dots of coating on cake pops to attach sprinkles for nose. Apply coating to one side of each licorice piece; press onto cake pops for smile. Pipe dot of black frosting in each eye.

Busy Bees
Makes about 24 pops

½ baked and cooled 13×9-inch cake*
½ cup plus 2 tablespoons frosting
1 package (14 to 16 ounces) yellow candy coating
24 lollipop sticks
Foam block
Black decorator frosting
Black string licorice, cut into ¾-inch lengths

Prepare a cake from a mix according to package directions or use your favorite recipe. Cake must be cooled completely.

1. Line large baking sheet with waxed paper. Use hands to crumble cake into large bowl. (You should end up with fine crumbs and no large cake pieces remaining.)

2. Add frosting to cake crumbs; mix with hands until well blended. Shape mixture into 1½-inch balls (about 2 tablespoons cake mixture per ball); place on prepared baking sheet. Cover with plastic wrap; refrigerate at least 1 hour or freeze 10 minutes to firm.

3. Reserve 24 yellow candy coating discs for wings. Cut reserved discs in half, then cut small piece from each half to create flat edge.

4. When cake balls are firm, place remaining yellow candy coating in deep microwavable bowl. Melt according to package directions. Dip one lollipop stick about ½ inch into melted coating; insert stick into cake ball (no more than halfway through). Return to baking sheet in refrigerator to set. Repeat with remaining cake balls and sticks.

5. Working with one cake pop at a time, hold stick and dip cake ball into melted coating to cover completely, letting excess coating drip off. Rotate stick gently and/or tap stick on edge of bowl, if necessary, to remove excess coating. Place cake pop in foam block.

6. Pipe three stripes of black frosting around each cake pop. Dip toothpick in candy coating; place two dots of coating behind center stripe. Press reserved yellow disc halves, flat sides facing you, into coating for wings; hold in place until coating is set.

7. Pipe two dots of frosting at top of first stripe; attach two licorice pieces for antennae and hold in place until set. Pipe eyes and smile with black frosting.

Nice Mice

Makes about 24 pops

½ baked and cooled 13×9-inch cake*
½ cup plus 2 tablespoons frosting
1 package (14 to 16 ounces) chocolate candy coating
24 lollipop sticks
  Foam block
  Additional chocolate candy coating discs
  White round candies
  Small pink candies, candy-coated mini chocolate pieces or decors
  Black decorator frosting

*Prepare a cake from a mix according to package directions or use your favorite recipe. Cake must be cooled completely.

1. Line large baking sheet with waxed paper. Use hands to crumble cake into large bowl. (You should end up with fine crumbs and no large cake pieces remaining.)

2. Add frosting to cake crumbs; mix with hands until well blended. Shape mixture into 1½-inch balls (about 2 tablespoons cake mixture per ball); place on prepared baking sheet. Cover with plastic wrap; refrigerate at least 1 hour or freeze 10 minutes to firm.

3. When cake balls are firm, place candy coating in deep microwavable bowl. Melt according to package directions. Dip one lollipop stick about ½ inch into melted coating; insert stick into cake ball (no more than halfway through). Return cake pop to baking sheet in refrigerator to set. Repeat with remaining cake balls and sticks.

4. Working with one cake pop at a time, hold stick and dip cake ball into melted coating to cover completely, letting excess coating drip off. Rotate stick gently and/or tap stick on edge of bowl, if necessary, to remove excess coating. Place cake pop in foam block. Immediately attach two chocolate discs to top of pop for ears while coating is still wet; hold in place until coating is set.

5. Dip toothpick in candy coating; place two dots of coating on cake pops to attach white candies for eyes. Add dot of coating and pink candy for nose. Pipe dot of black frosting in each eye.

Tip: To add tails, roll small pieces of chewy chocolate candies between your hands into very thin ropes. Attach to mice using melted candy coating.

Pink Pig Pops
Makes about 24 pops

½ baked and cooled 13×9-inch cake*
½ cup plus 2 tablespoons frosting
  Pink chewy fruit candy squares or taffy strips
1 package (14 to 16 ounces) pink candy coating
24 lollipop sticks
  Foam block
  Mini semisweet chocolate chips
  Pink fruit-flavored pastel candy wafers
  Black decorator frosting

Prepare a cake from a mix according to package directions or use your favorite recipe. Cake must be cooled completely.

1. Line large baking sheet with waxed paper. Use hands to crumble cake into large bowl. (You should end up with fine crumbs and no large cake pieces remaining.)

2. Add frosting to cake crumbs; mix with hands until well blended. Shape mixture into 1½-inch balls (about 2 tablespoons cake mixture per ball); place on prepared baking sheet. Cover with plastic wrap; refrigerate at least 1 hour or freeze 10 minutes to firm.

3. Meanwhile, prepare ears. Working with one at a time, unwrap candy squares and microwave on LOW (30%) 5 to 8 seconds or until softened. Press candies between hands or on waxed paper to flatten to ⅛-inch thickness. Use scissors or paring knife to cut out triangles. Bend tips of ears, if desired.

4. When cake balls are firm, place candy coating in deep microwavable bowl. Melt according to package directions. Dip one lollipop stick about ½ inch into melted coating; insert stick into cake ball (no more than halfway through). Return cake pop to baking sheet in refrigerator to set. Repeat with remaining cake balls and sticks.

5. Working with one cake pop at a time, hold stick and dip cake ball into melted coating to cover completely, letting excess coating drip off. Rotate stick gently and/or tap stick on edge of bowl, if necessary, to remove excess coating. Place cake pop in foam block. Immediately attach two candy ears to top of pop while coating is still wet; hold in place until coating is set.

6. Dip toothpick in candy coating; place two dots of coating on cake pops to attach mini chips for eyes. (Cut off pointed tips of chips with knife so chips will lay flat.) Add dot of coating and candy wafer for nose. Pipe two dots of black frosting on each nose.

Tip: To add tails, roll small pieces of softened candy squares between your hands into thin ropes. Curl tails; attach to pigs using melted candy coating.

Funky Monkeys

Makes about 24 pops

½ baked and cooled 13×9-inch cake*
½ cup plus 2 tablespoons frosting
   Small chewy chocolate candies
 1 package (14 to 16 ounces) chocolate candy coating
24 lollipop sticks
   Foam block
   Brown candy-coated chocolate pieces
   Round yellow candies
   Black and yellow decorator frosting

Prepare a cake from a mix according to package directions or use your favorite recipe. Cake must be cooled completely.

1. Line large baking sheet with waxed paper. Use hands to crumble cake into large bowl. (You should end up with fine crumbs and no large cake pieces remaining.)

2. Add frosting to cake crumbs; mix with hands until well blended. Shape mixture into 1½-inch balls (about 2 tablespoons cake mixture per ball); place on prepared baking sheet. Cover with plastic wrap; refrigerate at least 1 hour or freeze 10 minutes to firm.

3. Meanwhile, prepare hair. Press and flatten chocolate candies into thin rectangles. (If candies are too stiff to flatten, microwave several seconds to soften.) Use scissors to make ¼-inch-long cuts across bottom (long) edge of candy. Fold candy into thirds or roll up candy so fringe is on top; separate and bend fringe pieces to create hair.

4. When cake balls are firm, place candy coating in deep microwavable bowl. Melt according to package directions. Dip one lollipop stick about ½ inch into melted coating; insert stick into cake ball (no more than halfway through). Return cake pop to baking sheet in refrigerator to set. Repeat with remaining cake balls and sticks.

5. Working with one cake pop at a time, hold stick and dip cake ball into melted coating to cover completely, letting excess coating drip off. Rotate stick gently and/or tap stick on edge of bowl, if necessary, to remove excess coating. Place cake pop in foam block. Immediately attach two chocolate pieces to sides of pop for ears while coating is still wet; hold in place until coating is set.

6. Dip toothpick in candy coating; place dot of coating in center of cake pops to attach yellow candy. Pipe two dots of black frosting above yellow candy for eyes; pipe smile on yellow candy. Pipe dot of yellow frosting in each ear. Dip toothpick in candy coating; place dot of coating on top of cake pops to attach hair. Hold in place until coating is set.

Tweet Treats

Makes about 24 pops

½ baked and cooled 13×9-inch cake*
½ cup plus 2 tablespoons frosting
Yellow and orange chewy fruit candy squares or taffy strips
1 package (14 to 16 ounces) yellow candy coating
24 lollipop sticks
Foam block
Black decorator frosting

Prepare a cake from a mix according to package directions or use your favorite recipe. Cake must be cooled completely.

1. Line large baking sheet with waxed paper. Use hands to crumble cake into large bowl. (You should end up with fine crumbs.)

2. Add frosting to cake crumbs; mix with hands until well blended. Shape mixture into 1½-inch balls (about 2 tablespoons cake mixture per ball); place on prepared baking sheet. Cover with plastic wrap; refrigerate at least 1 hour or freeze 10 minutes to firm.

3. Meanwhile, prepare decorations. Working with one at a time, unwrap yellow candy squares and microwave on LOW (30%) 5 to 8 seconds or until softened. Press candies between hands or on waxed paper to flatten to ⅛-inch thickness. Use scissors or paring knife to cut out triangles for wings and top feathers. Repeat procedure with orange candy squares, pressing candies thinner (¹⁄₁₆ inch) and cutting into smaller triangles for beaks.

4. When cake balls are firm, place candy coating in deep microwavable bowl. Melt according to package directions. Dip one lollipop stick about ½ inch into melted coating; insert stick into cake ball (no more than halfway through). Return cake pop to baking sheet in refrigerator to set. Repeat with remaining cake balls and sticks.

5. Working with one cake pop at a time, hold stick and dip cake ball into melted coating to cover completely, letting excess coating drip off. Rotate stick gently and/or tap stick on edge of bowl, if necessary, to remove excess coating. Place cake pop in foam block. Immediately attach two yellow triangles to sides of pop for wings while coating is still wet; hold in place until coating is set.

6. Dip toothpick in candy coating; place dots of coating on top of cake pops to attach top feathers. Add dots of coating and two orange triangles for beak. Pipe two dots of black frosting above beak for eyes.

Little Ladybugs

Makes about 24 pops

½ baked and cooled 13×9-inch cake*

½ cup plus 2 tablespoons frosting

1 package (14 to 16 ounces) red candy coating

24 lollipop sticks

Foam block

Dark chocolate-covered peanuts, caramels or other round candies (about ½ inch in diameter)

1½ cups semisweet chocolate chips

White and red decors or small candies

Chocolate sprinkles

*Prepare a cake from a mix according to package directions or use your favorite recipe. Cake must be cooled completely.

1. Line large baking sheet with waxed paper. Use hands to crumble cake into large bowl. (You should end up with fine crumbs and no large cake pieces remaining.)

2. Add frosting to cake crumbs; mix with hands until well blended. Shape mixture into 1½-inch balls (about 2 tablespoons cake mixture per ball); place on prepared baking sheet. Cover with plastic wrap; refrigerate at least 1 hour or freeze 10 minutes to firm.

3. When cake balls are firm, place candy coating in deep microwavable bowl. Melt according to package directions. Dip one lollipop stick about ½ inch into melted coating; insert stick into cake ball (no more than halfway through). Return cake pop to baking sheet in refrigerator to set. Repeat with remaining cake balls and sticks.

4. Working with one cake pop at a time, hold stick and dip cake ball into melted coating to cover completely, letting excess coating drip off. Rotate stick gently and/or tap stick on edge of bowl, if necessary, to remove excess coating. Place cake pop in foam block. Immediately attach chocolate-covered candy to front of pop for head while coating is still wet; hold in place until coating is set.

5. Place chocolate chips in small resealable food storage bag. Microwave on MEDIUM (50%) 1 minute. Knead bag; microwave 30 seconds to 1 minute or until chocolate is melted and smooth. Cut off small corner of bag; pipe stripe of chocolate down center of each cake pop starting from head. Pipe small circles of chocolate all over cake pop for ladybug spots.

6. Pipe two very small dots of chocolate (or use toothpick) on candy head; attach white decors for eyes using tweezers. Add dot of chocolate and red decor for mouth. Pipe two dots of chocolate above eyes; attach two chocolate sprinkles vertically for antennae. Pipe tiny dot of chocolate in center of each eye.

Teddy Bear Pops
Makes about 24 pops

½ baked and cooled 13×9-inch cake*
½ cup plus 2 tablespoons frosting
1 package (14 to 16 ounces) peanut butter candy coating
24 lollipop sticks
Foam block
1½ cups extra-large semisweet chocolate chips, divided
White chocolate chips
Mini semisweet chocolate chips

Prepare a cake from a mix according to package directions or use your favorite recipe. Cake must be cooled completely.

1. Line large baking sheet with waxed paper. Use hands to crumble cake into large bowl. (You should end up with fine crumbs and no large cake pieces remaining.)

2. Add frosting to cake crumbs; mix with hands until well blended. Shape mixture into 1½-inch balls (about 2 tablespoons cake mixture per ball); place on prepared baking sheet. Cover with plastic wrap; refrigerate at least 1 hour or freeze 10 minutes to firm.

3. When cake balls are firm, place candy coating in deep microwavable bowl. Melt according to package directions. Dip one lollipop stick about ½ inch into melted coating; insert stick into cake ball (no more than halfway through). Return cake pop to baking sheet in refrigerator to set. Repeat with remaining cake balls and sticks.

4. Working with one cake pop at a time, hold stick and dip cake ball into melted coating to cover completely, letting excess coating drip off. Rotate stick gently and/or tap stick on edge of bowl, if necessary, to remove excess coating. Place cake pop in foam block. Immediately attach two large chocolate chips to top of pop for ears while coating is still wet; hold in place until coating is set.

5. Dip toothpick in coating; place two dots of coating on cake pops to attach white chips for eyes. Add dot of coating and mini chocolate chip for nose.

6. When all pops have ears, eyes and noses, place remaining large chocolate chips in small resealable food storage bag. Microwave on MEDIUM (50%) 45 seconds. Knead bag; microwave 30 seconds to 1 minute or until chocolate is melted and smooth. Cut off small corner of bag; pipe mouths and pupils on bear faces.

Playtime Pops

Touchdown Treats
Makes about 24 pops

½ baked and cooled 13×9-inch cake*
½ cup plus 2 tablespoons frosting
1 package (14 to 16 ounces) chocolate candy coating
24 lollipop sticks
Foam block
White decorator frosting

Prepare a cake from a mix according to package directions or use your favorite recipe. Cake must be cooled completely.

1. Line large baking sheet with waxed paper. Use hands to crumble cake into large bowl. (You should end up with fine crumbs and no large cake pieces remaining.)

2. Add frosting to cake crumbs; mix with hands until well blended. Shape mixture into tapered oval footballs (about 2 tablespoons cake mixture per football); place on prepared baking sheet. Cover with plastic wrap; refrigerate at least 1 hour or freeze 10 minutes to firm.

3. When cake balls are firm, place candy coating in deep microwavable bowl. Melt according to package directions. Dip one lollipop stick about ½ inch into melted coating; insert stick into cake ball (no more than halfway through). Return cake pop to baking sheet in refrigerator to set. Repeat with remaining cake balls and sticks.

4. Working with one cake pop at a time, hold stick and dip cake ball into melted coating to cover completely, letting excess coating drip off. Rotate stick gently and/or tap stick on edge of bowl, if necessary, to remove excess coating. Place cake pop in foam block.

5. Pipe laces and lines on cake pops with white frosting.

Balloon Pops
Makes about 24 pops

½ baked and cooled 13×9-inch cake*
½ cup plus 2 tablespoons frosting
   Red, yellow or blue chewy fruit candy squares or taffy strips
1 package (14 to 16 ounces) red, yellow or blue candy coating
24 lollipop sticks
   Foam block

*Prepare a cake from a mix according to package directions or use your favorite recipe. Cake must be cooled completely.

1. Line large baking sheet with waxed paper. Use hands to crumble cake into large bowl. (You should end up with fine crumbs and no large cake pieces remaining.)

2. Add frosting to cake crumbs; mix with hands until well blended. Shape mixture into 1½-inch balls (about 2 tablespoons cake mixture per ball); place on prepared baking sheet. Cover with plastic wrap; refrigerate at least 1 hour or freeze 10 minutes to firm.

3. Meanwhile, prepare balloon knots. Unwrap candy squares; cut each into four pieces. Working with one piece at a time, microwave on LOW (30%) 5 seconds or until softened. Press candy between hands or on waxed paper to flatten and shape into ⅛-inch-thick circle. Use end of lollipop stick to poke hole in center of circle; bend circle into cone shape to resemble balloon knot.

4. When cake balls are firm, place candy coating in deep microwavable bowl. Melt according to package directions. Dip one lollipop stick about ½ inch into melted coating; insert stick into cake ball (no more than halfway through). Return cake pop to baking sheet in refrigerator to set. Repeat with remaining cake balls and sticks.

5. Working with one cake pop at a time, hold stick and dip cake ball into melted coating to cover completely, letting excess coating drip off. Rotate stick gently and/or tap stick on edge of bowl, if necessary, to remove excess coating. Place cake pop in foam block.

6. Dip toothpick in candy coating; place dots of coating around base of each cake pop where stick is attached. Slide candy balloon knot up stick and attach to base of cake pop; hold in place until coating is set.

Lucky Dice Pops

Makes about 24 pops

½ baked and cooled 13×9-inch cake*
½ cup plus 2 tablespoons frosting
1 package (14 to 16 ounces) white candy coating
24 lollipop sticks
Foam block
Black decorator frosting or black gel frosting

Prepare a cake from a mix according to package directions or use your favorite recipe. Cake must be cooled completely.

1. Line large baking sheet with waxed paper. Use hands to crumble cake into large bowl. (You should end up with fine crumbs and no large cake pieces remaining.)

2. Add frosting to cake crumbs; mix with hands until well blended. Shape mixture into 1½-inch balls (about 2 tablespoons cake mixture per ball); shape balls into squares. Place on prepared baking sheet. Cover with plastic wrap; refrigerate at least 1 hour or freeze 10 minutes to firm.

3. When cake balls are firm, place candy coating in deep microwavable bowl. Melt according to package directions. Dip one lollipop stick about ½ inch into melted coating; insert stick into cake ball (no more than halfway through). Return cake pop to baking sheet in refrigerator to set. Repeat with remaining cake balls and sticks.

4. Working with one cake pop at a time, hold stick and dip cake ball into melted coating to cover completely, letting excess coating drip off. Rotate stick gently and/or tap stick on edge of bowl, if necessary, to remove excess coating. Place cake pop in foam block.

5. Pipe dots on top and sides of cake pops with black frosting.

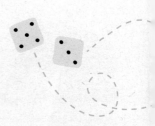

High-Flying Kites
Makes about 24 pops

½ baked and cooled 13×9-inch cake*
½ cup plus 2 tablespoons frosting
½ (14- to 16-ounce) package purple candy coating
½ (14- to 16-ounce) package green candy coating
24 lollipop sticks
    Foam block
    Yellow decorator frosting
    Assorted color decors or small candies
    Yellow string licorice

*Prepare a cake from a mix according to package directions or use your favorite recipe. Cake must be cooled completely.

1. Line large baking sheet with waxed paper. Use hands to crumble cake into large bowl. (You should end up with fine crumbs and no large cake pieces remaining.)

2. Add frosting to cake crumbs; mix with hands until well blended. Shape mixture into 1½-inch balls (about 2 tablespoons cake mixture per ball); shape balls into diamonds. Place on prepared baking sheet. Cover with plastic wrap; refrigerate at least 1 hour or freeze 10 minutes to firm.

3. When cake balls are firm, place candy coatings in separate deep microwavable bowls. Melt according to package directions. Dip one lollipop stick about ½ inch into melted coating; insert stick into cake ball (no more than halfway through). Return cake pop to baking sheet in refrigerator to set. Repeat with remaining cake balls and sticks.

4. Working with one cake pop at a time, hold stick and dip cake ball into melted coating to cover completely, letting excess coating drip off. Rotate stick gently and/or tap stick on edge of bowl, if necessary, to remove excess coating. Place cake pop in foam block.

5. Pipe crossbars on cake pops with yellow frosting. Dip toothpick in candy coating; place dots of coating on pops to attach decors as desired.

6. Cut licorice into desired lengths for kite tails. Attach licorice to back of cake pops using coating; hold in place until coating is set.

Home Run Pops
Makes about 24 pops

½ baked and cooled 13×9-inch cake*
½ cup plus 2 tablespoons frosting
1 package (14 to 16 ounces) white candy coating
24 lollipop sticks
Foam block
Red decorator frosting

Prepare a cake from a mix according to package directions or use your favorite recipe. Cake must be cooled completely.

1. Line large baking sheet with waxed paper. Use hands to crumble cake into large bowl. (You should end up with fine crumbs and no large cake pieces remaining.)

2. Add frosting to cake crumbs; mix with hands until well blended. Shape mixture into 1½-inch balls (about 2 tablespoons cake mixture per ball); place on prepared baking sheet. Cover with plastic wrap; refrigerate at least 1 hour or freeze 10 minutes to firm.

3. When cake balls are firm, place candy coating in deep microwavable bowl. Melt according to package directions. Dip one lollipop stick about ½ inch into melted coating; insert stick into cake ball (no more than halfway through). Return cake pop to baking sheet in refrigerator to set. Repeat with remaining cake balls and sticks.

4. Working with one cake pop at a time, hold stick and dip cake ball into melted coating to cover completely, letting excess coating drip off. Rotate stick gently and/or tap stick on edge of bowl, if necessary, to remove excess coating. Place cake pop in foam block.

5. Pipe seams on cake pops with red frosting.

Party Poppers
Makes about 24 pops

½ baked and cooled 13×9-inch cake*
½ cup plus 2 tablespoons frosting
½ (14- to 16-ounce) package blue candy coating
½ (14- to 16-ounce) package red candy coating
24 lollipop sticks
Foam block
Red and blue gumdrops or other round candies
Red and blue decorator frosting
Red and blue sprinkles and decors

*Prepare a cake from a mix according to package directions or use your favorite recipe. Cake must be cooled completely.

1. Line large baking sheet with waxed paper. Use hands to crumble cake into large bowl. (You should end up with fine crumbs and no large cake pieces remaining.)

2. Add frosting to cake crumbs; mix with hands until well blended. Shape mixture into 2½-inch-tall triangles (about 2 tablespoons cake mixture per triangle); place on prepared baking sheet. Cover with plastic wrap; refrigerate at least 1 hour or freeze 10 minutes to firm.

3. When cake balls are firm, place candy coatings in separate deep microwavable bowls. Melt according to package directions. Dip one lollipop stick about ½ inch into melted coating; insert stick into cake ball (no more than halfway through). Return cake pop to baking sheet in refrigerator to set. Repeat with remaining cake balls and sticks.

4. Working with one cake pop at a time, hold stick and dip cake ball into melted coating to cover completely, letting excess coating drip off. Rotate stick gently and/or tap stick on edge of bowl, if necessary, to remove excess coating. Place cake pop in foam block. Immediately attach gumdrop to top of pop while coating is still wet; hold in place until coating is set. (Or omit gumdrop and pipe decorator frosting on top of cake pop instead.)

5. Pipe decorator frosting along bottom of each cake pop. Pipe dots on cake pops with frosting, or dip toothpick in candy coating and place dots of coating on cake pops to attach sprinkles and decors.

Pretty Package Pops
Makes about 24 pops

½ baked and cooled 13×9-inch cake*
½ cup plus 2 tablespoons frosting
½ (14- to 16-ounce) package blue candy coating
½ (14- to 16-ounce) package purple candy coating
24 lollipop sticks
   Foam block
   Assorted color taffy and gummy strips
   Assorted color spice drops or gumdrops

Prepare a cake from a mix according to package directions or use your favorite recipe. Cake must be cooled completely.

1. Line large baking sheet with waxed paper. Use hands to crumble cake into large bowl. (You should end up with fine crumbs and no large cake pieces remaining.)

2. Add frosting to cake crumbs; mix with hands until well blended. Shape mixture into 1½-inch balls (about 2 tablespoons cake mixture per ball); shape balls into squares. Place on prepared baking sheet. Cover with plastic wrap; refrigerate at least 1 hour or freeze 10 minutes to firm.

3. When cake balls are firm, place candy coatings in separate deep microwavable bowls. Melt according to package directions. Dip one lollipop stick about ½ inch into melted coating; insert stick into cake ball (no more than halfway through). Return cake pop to baking sheet in refrigerator to set. Repeat with remaining cake balls and sticks.

4. Working with one cake pop at a time, hold stick and dip cake ball into melted coating to cover completely, letting excess coating drip off. Rotate stick gently and/or tap stick on edge of bowl, if necessary, to remove excess coating. Place cake pop in foam block.

5. Cut pieces of taffy or gummy strips with scissors to fit around cake pops for ribbons. Apply coating to back of taffy with toothpick; press taffy onto cake pops and hold until coating is set.

6. For candy bows, cut slits in top of spice drops (cut about halfway through candies). Separate cut pieces of spice drops, pressing them outward to resemble loops of bow. (For bigger bow, cut small pieces from additional spice drop and press them into center of bow.) Dip toothpick in candy coating; place dot of coating on top of cake pops to attach bows.

Holiday Pops

Sweetheart Pops
Makes about 24 pops

½ baked and cooled 13×9-inch cake*
½ cup plus 2 tablespoons frosting
1 package (14 to 16 ounces) pink candy coating
24 lollipop sticks
   Foam block
   White decors, sugar pearls or sprinkles

Prepare a cake from a mix according to package directions or use your favorite recipe. Cake must be cooled completely.

1. Line large baking sheet with waxed paper. Use hands to crumble cake into large bowl. (You should end up with fine crumbs and no large cake pieces remaining.)

2. Add frosting to cake crumbs; mix with hands until well blended. Shape mixture into 1½-inch-balls (about 2 tablespoons cake mixture per ball); shape balls into hearts. Place on prepared baking sheet. Cover with plastic wrap; refrigerate at least 1 hour or freeze 10 minutes to firm.

3. When cake balls are firm, place candy coating in deep microwavable bowl. Melt according to package directions. Dip one lollipop stick about ½ inch into melted coating; insert stick into cake ball (no more than halfway through). Return cake pop to baking sheet in refrigerator to set. Repeat with remaining cake balls and sticks.

4. Working with one cake pop at a time, hold stick and dip cake ball into melted coating to cover completely, letting excess coating drip off. Rotate stick gently and/or tap stick on edge of bowl, if necessary, to remove excess coating. Place cake pop in foam block.

5. Dip toothpick in candy coating; place dots of coating on cake pops to attach decors and sugar pearls.

Variation: For quicker decorating, use white decorator frosting instead of decors. Pipe dots, hearts or lines on cake pops as desired.

Sweet Swirly Pops
Makes about 24 pops

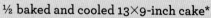

½ baked and cooled 13×9-inch cake*
½ cup plus 2 tablespoons frosting
½ (14- to 16-ounce) package chocolate candy coating
½ (14- to 16-ounce) package white candy coating
½ (14- to 16-ounce) package pink and/or red candy coating
24 lollipop sticks
    Foam block

*Prepare a cake from a mix according to package directions or use your favorite recipe. Cake must be cooled completely.

1. Line large baking sheet with waxed paper. Use hands to crumble cake into large bowl. (You should end up with fine crumbs and no large cake pieces remaining.)

2. Add frosting to cake crumbs; mix with hands until well blended. Shape mixture into 1½-inch balls (about 2 tablespoons cake mixture per ball); place on prepared baking sheet. Cover with plastic wrap; refrigerate at least 1 hour or freeze 10 minutes to firm.

3. When cake balls are firm, place candy coatings in separate deep microwavable bowls. Melt according to package directions. Dip one lollipop stick about ½ inch into melted coating; insert stick into cake ball (no more than halfway through). Return cake pop to baking sheet in refrigerator to set. Repeat with remaining cake balls and sticks.

4. Working with one cake pop at a time, hold stick and dip cake ball into melted chocolate or white coating to cover completely, letting excess coating drip off. Rotate stick gently and/or tap stick on edge of bowl, if necessary, to remove excess coating.

5. Immediately drizzle cake pop with melted pink or red coating using fork or spoon, turning pop constantly while drizzling. (For swirls to set smoothly in base coating, pop must be turned or shaken while drizzling, and drizzling must be done while base coating is still wet.) Place cake pop in foam block to set.

Tip: To make cake pops with two color swirls, drizzle cake pop with both colors immediately after dipping in base coating as directed in step 5.

Hoppin' Pops

Makes about 24 pops

½ baked and cooled 13×9-inch cake*
½ cup plus 2 tablespoons frosting
½ (14- to 16-ounce) package yellow candy coating
½ (14- to 16-ounce) package pink candy coating
24 lollipop sticks
    Foam block
    Mini semisweet chocolate chips
    White decorator frosting
    Granulated sugar

Prepare a cake from a mix according to package directions or use your favorite recipe. Cake must be cooled completely.

1. Line large baking sheet with waxed paper. Use hands to crumble cake into large bowl. (You should end up with fine crumbs and no large cake pieces remaining.)

2. Add frosting to cake crumbs; mix with hands until well blended. Shape mixture into bunny heads (about 2 tablespoons cake mixture per head); place on prepared baking sheet. Cover with plastic wrap; refrigerate at least 1 hour or freeze 10 minutes to firm.

3. When cake balls are firm, place candy coatings in separate deep microwavable bowls. Melt according to package directions. Dip one lollipop stick about ½ inch into melted coating; insert stick into cake ball (no more than halfway through). Return cake pop to baking sheet in refrigerator to set. Repeat with remaining cake balls and sticks.

4. Working with one cake pop at a time, hold stick and dip cake ball into melted coating to cover completely, letting excess coating drip off. Rotate stick gently and/or tap stick on edge of bowl, if necessary, to remove excess coating. Place cake pop in foam block. Immediately attach two mini chips to pop for eyes while coating is still wet.

5. Dip toothpick in candy coating; place dot of coating below eyes to attach additional mini chip for nose.

6. Pipe white frosting in center of each ear; sprinkle with sugar to coat. Brush off any excess sugar from cake pops.

Easter Egg Pops

Makes about 24 pops

½ baked and cooled 13×9-inch cake*
½ cup plus 2 tablespoons frosting
½ (14- to 16-ounce) package pink candy coating
½ (14- to 16-ounce) package yellow candy coating
24 lollipop sticks
   Foam block
   White, yellow or pink decorator frosting
   Pastel-colored decors, sugar pearls or sprinkles

Prepare a cake from a mix according to package directions or use your favorite recipe. Cake must be cooled completely.

1. Line large baking sheet with waxed paper. Use hands to crumble cake into large bowl. (You should end up with fine crumbs and no large cake pieces remaining.)

2. Add frosting to cake crumbs; mix with hands until well blended. Shape mixture into 1½-inch eggs (about 2 tablespoons cake mixture per egg); place on prepared baking sheet. Cover with plastic wrap; refrigerate at least 1 hour or freeze 10 minutes to firm.

3. When cake balls are firm, place candy coatings in separate deep microwavable bowls. Melt according to package directions. Dip one lollipop stick about ½ inch into melted coating; insert stick into cake ball (no more than halfway through). Return cake pop to baking sheet in refrigerator to set. Repeat with remaining cake balls and sticks.

4. Working with one cake pop at a time, hold stick and dip cake ball into melted coating to cover completely, letting excess coating drip off. Rotate stick gently and/or tap stick on edge of bowl, if necessary, to remove excess coating. Place cake pop in foam block.

5. Pipe lines on cake pops with decorator frosting. Dip toothpick in candy coating; place dots of coating on cake pops to attach decors and sugar pearls.

Earth Day Pops

Makes about 24 pops

½ baked and cooled 13×9-inch cake*
½ cup plus 2 tablespoons frosting
1 package (14 to 16 ounces) blue candy coating
½ package (14 to 16 ounces) green candy coating
24 lollipop sticks
Foam block

Prepare a cake from a mix according to package directions or use your favorite recipe. Cake must be cooled completely.

1. Line large baking sheet with waxed paper. Use hands to crumble cake into large bowl. (You should end up with fine crumbs and no large cake pieces remaining.)

2. Add frosting to cake crumbs; mix with hands until well blended. Shape mixture into 1½-inch balls (about 2 tablespoons cake mixture per ball); place on prepared baking sheet. Cover with plastic wrap; refrigerate at least 1 hour or freeze 10 minutes to firm.

3. When cake balls are firm, place candy coatings in separate deep microwavable bowls. Melt according to package directions. Dip one lollipop stick about ½ inch into melted blue coating; insert stick into cake ball (no more than halfway through). Return cake pop to baking sheet in refrigerator to set. Repeat with remaining cake balls and sticks.

4. Working with one cake pop at a time, hold stick and dip cake ball into melted blue coating to cover completely, letting excess coating drip off. Rotate stick gently and/or tap stick on edge of bowl, if necessary, to remove excess coating.

5. Immediately drizzle cake pop with melted green coating using fork or spoon, turning pop constantly while drizzling. (For green swirls to set smoothly in blue coating, pop must be turned or shaken while drizzling, and drizzling must be done while blue coating is still wet.) Place cake pop in foam block to set.

Pumpkin Patch Pops

Makes about 24 pops

½ baked and cooled 13×9-inch cake*
½ cup plus 2 tablespoons frosting
1½ packages (14 to 16 ounces each) orange candy coating
24 lollipop sticks
    Green gumdrops or spice drops
    Foam block

*Prepare a cake from a mix according to package directions or use your favorite recipe. Cake must be cooled completely.

1. Line large baking sheet with waxed paper. Use hands to crumble cake into large bowl. (You should end up with fine crumbs and no large cake pieces remaining.)

2. Add frosting to cake crumbs; mix with hands until well blended. Shape mixture into 1½-inch balls (about 2 tablespoons cake mixture per ball); flatten balls slightly to resemble pumpkin shape and make indentation in top of each ball for stem. Place on prepared baking sheet. Cover with plastic wrap; refrigerate at least 1 hour or freeze 10 minutes to firm.

3. When cake balls are firm, place candy coating in deep microwavable bowl. Melt according to package directions. Dip one lollipop stick about ½ inch into melted coating; insert stick into cake ball (no more than halfway through). Return cake pop to baking sheet in refrigerator to set. Repeat with remaining cake balls and sticks.

4. Cut gumdrops in half, if necessary, to create stems. Working with one cake pop at a time, hold stick and dip cake ball into melted coating to cover completely, letting excess coating drip off. Rotate stick gently and/or tap stick on edge of bowl, if necessary, to remove excess coating. Place cake pop in foam block. Immediately attach gumdrop to top of pop while coating is still wet; hold in place until coating is set.

5. Transfer remaining candy coating to small resealable food storage bag. (Reheat briefly in microwave if coating has hardened.) Cut off small corner of bag; pipe vertical lines on each cake pop from stem to stick. Pipe coating around stem, if desired.

Variation: You can use orange decorator frosting instead of candy coating to pipe the lines on the cake pops.

Boo Bites

Makes about 24 pops

½ baked and cooled 13×9-inch cake*
½ cup plus 2 tablespoons frosting
1 package (14 to 16 ounces) white candy coating
24 lollipop sticks
    Foam block
    Black decorator frosting or black gel frosting

Prepare a cake from a mix according to package directions or use your favorite recipe. Cake must be cooled completely.

1. Line large baking sheet with waxed paper. Use hands to crumble cake into large bowl. (You should end up with fine crumbs and no large cake pieces remaining.)

2. Add frosting to cake crumbs; mix with hands until well blended. Shape mixture into rounded triangles (about 2 tablespoons cake mixture per triangle), about 2 inches tall and with uneven or wavy edges to resemble ghosts. Place on prepared baking sheet. Cover with plastic wrap; refrigerate at least 1 hour or freeze 10 minutes to firm.

3. When cake balls are firm, place candy coating in deep microwavable bowl. Melt according to package directions. Dip one lollipop stick about ½ inch into melted coating; insert stick into cake ball (no more than halfway through). Return cake pop to baking sheet in refrigerator to set. Repeat with remaining cake balls and sticks.

4. Working with one cake pop at a time, hold stick and dip cake ball into melted coating to cover completely, letting excess coating drip off. Rotate stick gently and/or tap stick on edge of bowl, if necessary, to remove excess coating. Place cake pop in foam block.

5. Pipe eyes and mouths on cake pops with black frosting.

Reindeer Pops

Makes about 24 pops

½ baked and cooled 13×9-inch cake*
½ cup plus 2 tablespoons frosting
1 package (14 to 16 ounces) chocolate candy coating
24 lollipop sticks
48 small pretzel twists
   Foam block
   Semisweet chocolate chips
   Round white candies
   Red candy-coated chocolate pieces
   Black decorator frosting or black gel frosting

Prepare a cake from a mix according to package directions or use your favorite recipe. Cake must be cooled completely.

1. Line large baking sheet with waxed paper. Use hands to crumble cake into large bowl. (You should end up with fine crumbs and no large cake pieces remaining.)

2. Add frosting to cake crumbs; mix with hands until well blended. Shape mixture into rounded triangles or skull shape (about 2 tablespoons cake mixture per triangle); place on prepared baking sheet. Cover with plastic wrap; refrigerate at least 1 hour or freeze 10 minutes to firm.

3. When cake balls are firm, place candy coating in deep microwavable bowl. Melt according to package directions. Dip one lollipop stick about ½ inch into melted coating; insert stick into cake ball (no more than halfway through). Return cake pop to baking sheet in refrigerator to set. Repeat with remaining cake balls and sticks.

4. Break off one section from each pretzel twist; set aside.

5. Working with one cake pop at a time, hold stick and dip cake ball into melted coating to cover completely, letting excess coating drip off. Rotate stick gently and/or tap stick on edge of bowl, if necessary, to remove excess coating. Place cake pop in foam block. Immediately attach two pretzel twists to top of pop for antlers while coating is still wet; hold in place until coating is set.

6. Dip toothpick in candy coating; place two dots of coating on either side of pretzel twists to attach chocolate chips for ears. Add two dots of coating and white candies for eyes. Add dot of coating and chocolate piece for nose. Pipe dot of black frosting in center of each eye.

Frosty's Friends
Makes about 16 pops

½ baked and cooled 13×9-inch cake*

½ cup plus 2 tablespoons frosting

1 package (14 to 16 ounces) white candy coating

16 lollipop sticks

Foam block

Orange candy-coated sunflower seeds or chocolate pieces

Assorted color decors and candy dots

Black decorator frosting or black gel frosting

Assorted color taffy, gummy strings or string licorice

Assorted color gumdrops, candy discs and chocolate kisses

Prepare a cake from a mix according to package directions or use your favorite recipe. Cake must be cooled completely.

1. Line large baking sheet with waxed paper. Use hands to crumble cake into large bowl. (You should end up with fine crumbs and no large cake pieces remaining.)

2. Add frosting to cake crumbs; mix with hands until well blended. Shape mixture into 24 (1½-inch) balls (about 2 tablespoons cake mixture per ball); place 16 balls on prepared baking sheet. Divide each of remaining 8 balls in half; shape into smaller balls for heads and place on baking sheet. Cover with plastic wrap; refrigerate at least 1 hour or freeze 10 minutes to firm.

3. When cake balls are firm, place candy coating in deep microwavable bowl. Melt according to package directions. Dip one lollipop stick about 1 inch into melted coating; insert stick through larger cake ball so ½ inch of stick comes out top of cake ball. Dip end of stick in melted coating again; insert stick into smaller cake ball to create snowman head. (Cake balls should be touching.) Return cake pop to baking sheet in refrigerator to set. Repeat with remaining cake balls and sticks.

4. Working with one cake pop at a time, hold stick and dip cake balls into melted coating to cover completely, letting excess coating drip off. Rotate stick gently and/or tap stick on edge of bowl, if necessary, to remove excess coating. Place cake pop in foam block.

5. Cut orange candies in half for noses. Dip toothpick in candy coating; place dot of coating on cake pops to attach candy nose. Attach decors to snowman bodies for buttons. Pipe eyes and mouths with black frosting.

6. Cut or stretch taffy or gummy strings into long thin pieces for scarves. Carefully tie scarves around snowman necks.

7. Create hats using candies, decors and licorice as shown in photo. Attach hats to snowman heads using dots of coating.

Tip: For more elaborate scarves, cut lengths of taffy or gummy strings and braid them together. Cut the edges of the candies to resemble fringe.

Ornament Pops

Makes about 24 pops

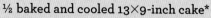

½ baked and cooled 13×9-inch cake*

½ cup plus 2 tablespoons frosting

1 package (14 to 16 ounces) white candy coating

24 lollipop sticks

Foam block

Red or yellow string licorice, cut into 1½-inch lengths

Red and green gumdrops or gummy candies

Assorted color candies, sprinkles, decors, sugar pearls and sparkling sugar

Red, white and green decorator frosting

Prepare a cake from a mix according to package directions or use your favorite recipe. Cake must be cooled completely.

1. Line large baking sheet with waxed paper. Use hands to crumble cake into large bowl. (You should end up with fine crumbs and no large cake pieces remaining.)

2. Add frosting to cake crumbs; mix with hands until well blended. Shape mixture into 1½-inch balls (about 2 tablespoons cake mixture per ball); place on prepared baking sheet. Cover with plastic wrap; refrigerate at least 1 hour or freeze 10 minutes to firm.

3. When cake balls are firm, place candy coating in deep microwavable bowl. Melt according to package directions. Dip one lollipop stick about ½ inch into melted coating; insert stick into cake ball (no more than halfway through). Return cake pop to baking sheet in refrigerator to set. Repeat with remaining cake balls and sticks.

4. Working with one cake pop at a time, hold stick and dip cake ball into melted coating to cover completely, letting excess coating drip off. Rotate stick gently and/or tap stick on edge of bowl, if necessary, to remove excess coating. Place cake pop in foam block. Immediately push both ends of licorice piece into top of pop to form hanger while coating is still wet; hold in place until coating is set. (Or press gumdrop or other candy into top of pop.)

5. Decorate cake pops with candies, sprinkles, decors, sugar pearls and sugar, using coating to attach decorations. Pipe lines and dots on cake pops with decorator frosting.

Jolly Pops

Makes about 24 pops

½ baked and cooled 13×9-inch cake*
½ cup plus 2 tablespoons frosting
1 package (14 to 16 ounces) red candy coating
24 lollipop sticks
Foam block
White candies, gumdrops or mini marshmallows
White decorator frosting

Prepare a cake from a mix according to package directions or use your favorite recipe. Cake must be cooled completely.

1. Line large baking sheet with waxed paper. Use hands to crumble cake into large bowl. (You should end up with fine crumbs and no large cake pieces remaining.)

2. Add frosting to cake crumbs; mix with hands until well blended. Shape mixture into 2½-inch-tall triangles (about 2 tablespoons cake mixture per triangle); place on prepared baking sheet. Cover with plastic wrap; refrigerate at least 1 hour or freeze 10 minutes to firm.

3. When cake balls are firm, place candy coating in deep microwavable bowl. Melt according to package directions. Dip one lollipop stick about ½ inch into melted coating; insert stick into cake ball (no more than halfway through). Return cake pop to baking sheet in refrigerator to set. Repeat with remaining cake balls and sticks.

4. Working with one cake pop at a time, hold stick and dip cake ball into melted coating to cover completely, letting excess coating drip off. Rotate stick gently and/or tap stick on edge of bowl, if necessary, to remove excess coating. Place cake pop in foam block. Immediately attach candy to top of pop while coating is still wet; hold in place until coating is set.

5. Pipe white frosting along bottom of each cake pop.

Mini Chocolate Whoopie Pies
Makes about 2 dozen sandwiches

- 1¾ cups all-purpose flour
- ½ cup unsweetened Dutch process cocoa powder
- ¾ teaspoon baking powder
- ½ teaspoon baking soda
- ½ teaspoon salt
- 1 cup packed brown sugar
- 1 cup (2 sticks) butter, softened, divided
- 1 egg
- 1½ teaspoons vanilla, divided
- 1 cup milk
- 1 cup marshmallow creme
- 1 cup powdered sugar

1. Preheat oven to 350°F. Line cookie sheets with parchment paper. Sift flour, cocoa, baking powder, baking soda and salt into medium bowl.

2. Beat brown sugar and ½ cup butter in large bowl with electric mixer at medium-high speed about 3 minutes or until light and fluffy. Beat in egg and 1 teaspoon vanilla until well blended. Alternately add flour mixture and milk, beating at low speed after each addition until smooth and well blended. Drop dough by heaping teaspoonfuls 2 inches apart onto prepared cookie sheets.

3. Bake 8 to 10 minutes or until cookies are puffed and tops spring back when lightly touched. Cool cookies on cookie sheets 10 minutes; remove to wire racks to cool completely.

4. Meanwhile, prepare filling. Beat remaining ½ cup butter, ½ teaspoon vanilla, marshmallow creme and powdered sugar in large bowl with electric mixer at high speed 2 minutes or until light and fluffy.

5. Spoon heaping teaspoon filling onto flat side of one cookie; top with second cookie. Repeat with remaining cookies and filling.

Ginger Molasses Spice Cookies
Makes about 12 dozen cookies

    2 cups all-purpose flour
1½ teaspoons ground ginger
  1 teaspoon baking soda
  ½ teaspoon salt
  ½ teaspoon ground cinnamon
  ½ teaspoon ground cloves
1¼ cups sugar, divided
  ¾ cup (1½ sticks) butter, softened
  ¼ cup molasses
  1 egg

1. Preheat oven to 375°F. Combine flour, ginger, baking soda, salt, cinnamon and cloves in medium bowl.

2. Beat 1 cup sugar and butter in large bowl with electric mixer at medium speed until light and fluffy. Add molasses and egg; beat until well blended. Gradually beat in flour mixture at low speed just until blended.

3. Place remaining ¼ cup sugar in shallow bowl. Shape dough by ½ teaspoonfuls into balls; roll in sugar to coat. Place 1 inch apart on ungreased cookie sheets.

4. Bake 7 to 8 minutes or until almost set. Cool cookies on cookie sheets 2 minutes; remove to wire racks to cool completely.

Brownie Buttons
Makes about 2 dozen brownies

½ cup (1 stick) butter
2 squares (1 ounce each) unsweetened chocolate
1 cup sugar
2 eggs, at room temperature
½ cup all-purpose flour
¼ teaspoon salt
1 teaspoon vanilla
½ cup semisweet chocolate chips
¼ cup whipping cream
Small chocolate nonpareil candies

1. Preheat oven to 325°F. Spray 8-inch square baking pan with nonstick cooking spray.

2. Melt butter and chocolate in small heavy saucepan over low heat. Remove from heat; gradually stir in sugar. Beat in eggs, one at a time, until blended. Stir in flour and salt. Stir in vanilla. Spread batter evenly in prepared pan.

3. Bake 25 to 28 minutes or until firm in center and toothpick inserted into center comes out with fudgy crumbs. Cool completely in pan on wire rack; refrigerate until chilled before cutting.

4. Use 1¼-inch round cookie or biscuit cutter to cut out circles from brownies. Place brownies on wire rack set over waxed paper.

5. Place chocolate chips in small heatproof bowl. Microwave cream on HIGH 1 minute or just until simmering; pour over chocolate chips. Let stand 1 minute; stir until smooth. Let stand several minutes to thicken slightly; pour mixture over tops of brownies. Place candy in center of each brownie.

Little Oatmeal Cookies

Makes about 6 dozen cookies

¾ cup all-purpose flour
½ teaspoon baking soda
½ teaspoon ground cinnamon
¼ teaspoon salt
½ cup (1 stick) butter, softened
½ cup packed brown sugar
¼ cup granulated sugar
1 egg
1 teaspoon vanilla
1½ cups quick or old-fashioned oats
½ cup raisins

1. Preheat oven to 350°F. Combine flour, baking soda, cinnamon and salt in medium bowl.

2. Beat butter, brown sugar and granulated sugar in large bowl with electric mixer at medium speed until creamy. Add egg and vanilla; beat until well blended. Gradually beat in flour mixture at low speed until well blended. Stir in oats and raisins until blended.

3. Drop dough by scant teaspoonfuls 2 inches apart onto ungreased cookie sheets.

4. Bake 7 to 8 minutes or just until edges are lightly browned. Cool cookies on cookie sheets 1 minute; remove to wire racks to cool completely.

Pumpkin Whoopie Minis
Makes about 2½ dozen sandwiches

1¾ cups all-purpose flour
2 teaspoons pumpkin pie spice
1 teaspoon baking powder
1 teaspoon baking soda
1 teaspoon salt, divided
1 cup packed brown sugar
½ cup (1 stick) butter, softened, divided
1 cup canned pumpkin
2 eggs, lightly beaten
¼ cup vegetable oil
1 teaspoon vanilla, divided
4 ounces cream cheese, softened
1½ cups powdered sugar

1. Preheat oven to 350°F. Line cookie sheets with parchment paper. Combine flour, pumpkin pie spice, baking powder, baking soda and ¾ teaspoon salt in medium bowl.

2. Beat brown sugar and ¼ cup butter in large bowl with electric mixer at medium speed until creamy. Beat in pumpkin, eggs, oil and ½ teaspoon vanilla until well blended. Beat in flour mixture at low speed just until blended. Drop dough by teaspoonfuls 2 inches apart onto prepared cookie sheets.

3. Bake 10 to 12 minutes or until springy to the touch. Cool cookies on cookie sheets 5 minutes; remove to wire racks to cool completely.

4. Meanwhile, prepare filling. Beat cream cheese and remaining ¼ cup butter in medium bowl with electric mixer until smooth and creamy. Beat in remaining ½ teaspoon vanilla and ¼ teaspoon salt until blended. Gradually add powdered sugar; beat until light and fluffy.

5. Spoon heaping teaspoon filling onto flat side of one cookie; top with second cookie. Repeat with remaining cookies and filling. Store cookies in airtight container in refrigerator.

Two-Bite Chocolate Chip Cookies

Makes about 14 dozen cookies

1¼ cups all-purpose flour
½ teaspoon baking soda
¼ teaspoon salt
½ cup (1 stick) butter, softened
½ cup packed light brown sugar
¼ cup granulated sugar
1 egg
1 teaspoon vanilla
1¼ cups mini semisweet chocolate chips
   Sea salt (optional)

1. Preheat oven to 350°F. Combine flour, baking soda and salt in medium bowl.

2. Beat butter, brown sugar and granulated sugar in large bowl with electric mixer at medium speed until light and fluffy. Beat in egg and vanilla until blended. Add flour mixture; beat at low speed until well blended. Stir in chocolate chips.

3. Drop dough by ½ teaspoonfuls 1 inch apart onto ungreased cookie sheets. Sprinkle very lightly with sea salt, if desired.

4. Bake 6 to 7 minutes or just until edges are golden brown. (Centers of cookies will be very light and will not look done.) Cool cookies on cookie sheets 2 minutes; remove to wire racks to cool completely.

Tiny Peanut Butter Sandwiches
Makes 6 to 7 dozen sandwiches

1¼ cups all-purpose flour
½ teaspoon baking powder
½ teaspoon baking soda
¼ teaspoon salt
½ cup (1 stick) butter, softened
½ cup granulated sugar
½ cup packed brown sugar
½ cup creamy peanut butter
1 egg
1 teaspoon vanilla
1 cup semisweet chocolate chips
½ cup whipping cream

1. Preheat oven to 350°F. Combine flour, baking powder, baking soda and salt in medium bowl.

2. Beat butter, granulated sugar and brown sugar in large bowl with electric mixer at medium speed until light and fluffy. Beat in peanut butter, egg and vanilla until well blended. Gradually beat in flour mixture at low speed until blended.

3. Shape dough by ½ teaspoonfuls into balls; place 1 inch apart on ungreased cookie sheets. Flatten balls slightly in criss-cross pattern with tines of fork.

4. Bake 6 minutes or just until set. Cool cookies on cookie sheets 4 minutes; remove to wire racks to cool completely.

5. Meanwhile, prepare filling. Place chocolate chips in medium heatproof bowl. Microwave cream on HIGH 2 minutes or just until simmering; pour over chocolate chips. Let stand 2 minutes; stir until smooth. Let stand 10 minutes or until filling thickens to desired consistency.

6. Spread scant teaspoon filling on flat side of one cookie; top with second cookie. Repeat with remaining cookies and filling.

Chocolate Chip S'More Bites

Makes about 4 dozen s'mores

1 package (about 16 ounces) refrigerated chocolate chip cookie dough
¾ cup semisweet chocolate chips
¼ cup plus 2 tablespoons whipping cream
½ cup marshmallow creme
½ cup sour cream

1. Preheat oven to 325°F. Spray 13×9-inch baking pan with nonstick cooking spray.

2. Press cookie dough into prepared pan, using damp hands to spread dough into even layer and cover bottom of pan. (Layer of dough will be very thin.) Bake 20 minutes or until light golden brown and just set. Cool in pan on wire rack.

3. Meanwhile, place chocolate chips in medium heatproof bowl. Microwave cream on HIGH 1 minute or just until simmering; pour over chocolate chips. Let stand 2 minutes; stir until smooth. Let stand 10 minutes or until mixture thickens.

4. Combine marshmallow creme and sour cream in small bowl until smooth.

5. Cut bars into 1¼-inch squares with sharp knife. For each s'more, spread scant teaspoon chocolate mixture on bottom of one square; spread scant teaspoon marshmallow mixture on bottom of second square. Press together to form s'mores.

Cute Little Cupcakes

Tangy Raspberry Minis
Makes 24 mini cupcakes

   1 cup all-purpose flour
 ½ teaspoon baking powder
 ½ teaspoon baking soda
 ½ cup granulated sugar
 ¼ cup (½ stick) butter, softened
   1 egg
 ½ teaspoon vanilla
 ½ cup buttermilk
24 fresh raspberries
   2 tablespoons coarse sugar
   2 cups powdered sugar
   6 to 9 tablespoons milk, divided

1. Preheat oven to 350°F. Line 24 mini (1¾-inch) muffin cups with paper baking cups; spray with nonstick cooking spray.

2. Whisk flour, baking powder and baking soda in small bowl. Beat granulated sugar and butter in large bowl with electric mixer at medium speed until creamy. Add egg and vanilla; beat until blended. Add flour mixture and buttermilk; beat at low speed just until combined.

3. Spoon batter evenly into prepared muffin cups. Place 1 raspberry on top of batter in each cup. Sprinkle evenly with coarse sugar.

4. Bake 15 minutes or until golden brown. Cool cupcakes in pans 5 minutes; remove to wire racks to cool completely.

5. Whisk powdered sugar and 6 tablespoons milk in medium bowl until smooth. Add remaining milk, 1 tablespoon at a time, to make pourable glaze. Drizzle over cupcakes.

Chocolate Caramel Bites

Makes 36 mini cupcakes

1 cup sugar
¾ cup plus 2 tablespoons all-purpose flour
½ cup unsweetened cocoa powder
¾ teaspoon baking soda
¾ teaspoon baking powder
½ teaspoon salt
½ cup plus 2 tablespoons whole milk, divided
¼ cup vegetable oil
1 egg
½ cup boiling water
24 caramels (about 7 ounces)
1 cup semisweet chocolate chips
Colored decors (optional)

1. Preheat oven to 350°F. Line 36 mini (1¾-inch) muffin cups with paper baking cups.

2. Whisk sugar, flour, cocoa, baking soda, baking powder and salt in medium bowl. Beat ½ cup milk, oil and egg in large bowl with electric mixer at medium speed until well blended. Add sugar mixture; beat 2 minutes. Add water; beat at low speed until blended. (Batter will be thin.) Pour into prepared muffin cups, filling three-fourths full.

3. Bake 8 minutes. Meanwhile, combine caramels and remaining 2 tablespoons milk in medium microwavable bowl. Microwave on HIGH 1½ minutes; stir. Microwave 1 minute or until caramels are completely melted.

4. Spoon ½ teaspoon caramel sauce over each partially baked cupcake. Bake 4 minutes or until toothpick inserted near edges of cupcakes comes out clean. Cool cupcakes in pans 10 minutes; remove to wire racks to cool completely.

5. Place chocolate chips in small microwavable bowl. Microwave on HIGH 1 minute; stir. Microwave at additional 15-second intervals until chocolate is melted. Reheat remaining caramel sauce in microwave until melted; drizzle chocolate and caramel sauce over cupcakes. Top with decors, if desired.

Carrot Cake Minis
Makes 36 mini cupcakes

    1 cup packed brown sugar
    ¾ cup plus 2 tablespoons all-purpose flour
    1 teaspoon baking soda
    ½ teaspoon salt
    ½ teaspoon ground cinnamon
    ¼ teaspoon ground nutmeg
    ⅛ teaspoon ground cloves
    ½ cup canola oil
    2 eggs
    1½ cups lightly packed grated carrots
    ½ teaspoon vanilla
      Cream Cheese Frosting (recipe follows)
      Toasted shredded coconut (optional)

1. Preheat oven to 350°F. Line 36 mini (1¾-inch) muffin cups with paper baking cups.

2. Whisk brown sugar, flour, baking soda, salt, cinnamon, nutmeg and cloves in large bowl. Stir in oil until blended. Add eggs, one at a time, stirring until blended after each addition. Stir in carrots and vanilla. Spoon batter evenly into prepared muffin cups.

3. Bake 15 minutes or until toothpick inserted into centers comes out clean. Cool cupcakes in pans 5 minutes; remove to wire racks to cool completely.

4. Meanwhile, prepare Cream Cheese Frosting. Frost cupcakes. Sprinkle with coconut, if desired. Store covered in refrigerator.

Cream Cheese Frosting: Beat 1 package (8 ounces) softened cream cheese and ¼ cup (½ stick) softened butter in medium bowl with electric mixer at medium-high speed until creamy. Beat in ¼ teaspoon salt and ¼ teaspoon vanilla. Gradually beat in 1½ cups sifted powdered sugar until well blended. Makes about 3 cups.

Tip: Use a food processor to quickly grate the carrots for this recipe. Use the metal blade and pulse the carrots until they are evenly grated.

Crispy Cupcakes
Makes 1½ dozen mini cupcakes

¼ cup (½ stick) plus 2 tablespoons butter, divided
1 package (10½ ounces) marshmallows
½ cup creamy peanut butter
6 cups crisp rice cereal
1 cup bittersweet or semisweet chocolate chips
1½ cups powdered sugar
¼ cup milk

1. Spray 13×9-inch baking pan with nonstick cooking spray. Microwave 2 tablespoons butter in large microwavable bowl on HIGH 30 seconds or until melted. Add marshmallows; stir until coated with butter. Microwave on HIGH 1 minute; stir. Microwave 45 seconds; stir until melted. Stir in peanut butter until well blended. Add cereal; stir until blended.

2. Spread mixture in prepared pan, using waxed paper to spread and press into even layer. Let stand 10 to 15 minutes or until set.

3. Meanwhile, place remaining ¼ cup butter and chocolate chips in medium microwavable bowl. Microwave on HIGH 40 seconds; stir. Microwave at additional 15-second intervals until melted and smooth. Gradually beat in powdered sugar and milk until well blended. Refrigerate until ready to use.

4. Spray 1½-inch round cookie or biscuit cutter with nonstick cooking spray; cut out 36 circles from cereal bars. Place small dab of frosting on top of 18 circles; top with remaining 18 circles, pressing down firmly to seal. Place "cupcakes" in paper baking cups, if desired. Pipe or spread frosting on cupcakes.